STOREHOUSES OF E

Liverpool's Historic Warehouses

Published by English Heritage, 23 Savile Row, London W1S 2ET
www.english-heritage.org.uk
English Heritage is the Government's statutory adviser on all aspects of the historic environment.

First published 2004

ISBN 1 873592 80 9
Product code 50920

British Library Cataloguing in Publication Data
A CIP catalogue record for this book is available from the British Library.

The National Monuments Record is the public archive of English Heritage. For more information
contact NMR Enquiry and Research Services, National Monuments Record Centre, Kemble Drive,
Swindon SN2 2GZ; telephone 01793 414600.

Brought to publication by René Rodgers and Andrew McLaren, Publishing, English Heritage,
Kemble Drive, Swindon SN2 2GZ

Edited by Delia Gaze
Page layout by George Hammond
Printed in the United Kingdom by Hawthornes

Liverpool City Council made a financial contribution towards the publication of this book.

STOREHOUSES OF EMPIRE

Liverpool's Historic Warehouses

Colum Giles and Bob Hawkins

ENGLISH HERITAGE

The City of Liverpool

Contents

Frontispiece *The converted warehouse at 15 Argyle Street.* *[AA041748]*

Acknowledgements

The authors would like to thank a number of individuals for assistance in the preparation of this booklet: Joseph Sharples and Richard Pollard of the Buildings of England, Liverpool project; Glynn Marsden of Liverpool City Council; John Stonard, Malcolm Cooper, Martin Cherry and Peter Guillery of English Heritage; Dr Adrian Jarvis of Merseyside Maritime Museum; the staff of Liverpool Record Office and Lancashire Record Office; Mr Eric Leatherbarrow, Port of Liverpool; and the owners and occupiers of warehouses in the city. Allan Adams, Garry Corbett, Ian Goodall, Adam Menuge, Simon Taylor and Nicola Wray of English Heritage provided assistance with fieldwork. The photographs were taken by Tony Perry, Peter Williams, James O Davies and Shaun Watts; the graphics were created by Tony Berry and Allan Adams. Administrative work was carried out by Ursula Dugard-Craig and Gillian Green. Figure 32 is reproduced with the consent of Edmund Kirby & Sons, Surveyors and Architects, India Buildings, Liverpool, and King Street, Manchester, from drawings in the Culshaw Collection at Lancashire Record Office (DDX 162).

Foreword

Liverpool, the 'maritime mercantile city', was inscribed on to the UNESCO list of World Heritage Sites in July 2004, a fitting recognition of the role that it has played in the development of a global trading network. Of all the building types present in Liverpool, warehouses are perhaps most emblematic of the city's history, for these buildings handled the trade that brought prosperity to the region. Once numbering hundreds, but now much fewer in number, they range from the well known – the monumental warehouses around Albert Dock – to the small and often overlooked buildings encountered throughout the central area and in other parts of the city.

The surviving warehouses are of great historical significance and collectively they give a special character to Liverpool. For English Heritage and Liverpool City Council, partners in the Historic Environment of Liverpool Project, this book has a dual aim. It seeks to promote better awareness of the important contribution that warehouses make to the city's historic environment. It also addresses the conservation challenges presented today in a Liverpool that, after slumbering for too long, is changing rapidly through economic regeneration, a trend reinforced by its selection as European Capital of Culture for 2008. Change is undoubtedly needed to restore the city's economy and pride, and there is much to build on. Good conservation, based on thorough understanding, will ensure that Liverpool remains a highly distinctive place. Success depends upon partnership with the private sector and on promoting good practice. This book, by defining the character and significance of a highly distinctive Liverpool building type and by outlining approaches to managing change, signals the commitment of both our organisations to achieve Liverpool's 21st-century renaissance.

Sir Neil Cossons
Chairman, English Heritage

Councillor Mike Storey
Leader, Liverpool City Council

CHAPTER 1

The development of Liverpool

Never was there a town in Europe which sprang from such poverty and insignificance to such opulence and importance, in so short a time.

Gawthrop 1861, 29

Some of the world's great cities are united in the popular mind with their river, and for reasons both ancient and modern Liverpool and the Mersey are inseparable (Fig 1). The relationship is not the same as that which we see in cities such as Paris, which develop on both banks of their river and where bridging points concentrate life and traffic on the waterfront. Instead, the great muddy river, too broad to span, runs past rather than through the city. But the Mersey is the reason for Liverpool's existence. Treacherous, fast flowing, with a huge tidal range, it nevertheless formed part of the chain that carried the trade of the world, linking large parts of northern and midland England with markets and sources of supply across the globe. For centuries, this traffic passed through Liverpool, the landing point for imports and the port of dispatch for goods sent overseas or around the coast (Fig 2). By the mid-19th century, Liverpool was far and away the dominant port for exports, handling 45 per cent of the United Kingdom total by value.

Fig 1 *(right) The Liverpool waterfront today, with the 'Three Graces': the Royal Liver Building (1908–10) to the left, the Cunard Shipping Company Offices (1914–16) in the centre, and the Mersey Docks and Harbour Company Offices (1907) to the right.* [AA029230]

Fig 2 *The Liverpool waterfront in the age of sail and steam: Samuel Walters,* The Port of Liverpool, *1873. [National Museums, Liverpool (The Walker)]*

Fig 3 *Liverpool's trading network: focused on the North Atlantic triangle, it extended to South America and Asia.*

Most major ports and towns had large numbers of warehouses, serving both inland and overseas trade and the everyday requirements of local or regional markets. Some towns display impressive collections of warehouses: Gloucester has huge buildings, clustered around its canal basin, that were constructed to store iron and grain; and in Manchester there developed a particular type of warehouse – the cotton packing and shipping warehouse – to serve the region's principal manufacturing industry. Liverpool is different to these and all other English towns. Unlike Bristol and Hull, it had an undistinguished role in national history before the 18th century; unlike Manchester, it did not develop a large industrial economy. Liverpool developed to serve a growing national and international trading network and for many decades handled more of the cargoes of Great Britain's maritime empire even than London. Here, therefore, the warehouse represents the essential function of the city and nowhere else can the evolution of this important building type be studied in such depth from surviving buildings.

Liverpool's rise from a fishing village to a port of global importance began in the Middle Ages, based on trade with Ireland and Scotland. By the 16th century, links had been established with the Atlantic ports of continental Europe in France, Spain and Portugal, and trade with North America began in the mid-17th century. Activity was, by later standards, modest: in 1700 just over 100 vessels entered the port. Horizons broadened in the 18th century, when the Atlantic triangle was developed, sending English manufactured goods and trinkets to Africa, slaves from there to plantations in the Caribbean and North America, and, last, rum, sugar and cotton back to England. At first, Bristol disputed supremacy in the Atlantic trade, but by the early 19th century Liverpool's status as the port for a rapidly developing industrial hinterland made it pre-eminent: in 1800 more than 4,000 vessels arrived here. The abolition of the slave trade in 1807 did little damage to the city's economy, for traffic grew with the addition of India, China and South America to Liverpool's network of trading links, and by 1871 more than 19,000 ships used the port (Fig 3).

A vast range of goods passed through the city. Raw cotton was for long the most significant import, but wool, spirits, tobacco, grain, meat,

sugar, foodstuffs, tea and metals were supplied to the region and, for some commodities, much of the country. The region's industries sent out cotton and wool textiles, engineering and chemical products, metal goods of all sorts, ceramics and glass; agriculture provided cheese and grain; and the extractive industries produced salt and, in large quantities, coal. In a period when most people's horizons were very limited, the bustling activity of the docks and the sometimes-exotic links indicated by the nature of the goods in transit were the subject of wonder. They also demonstrated how mercantile enterprise was the foundation of the city's wealth (Fig 4).

The port's growing trade was assisted by the development of a sophisticated system of port and transport facilities, many promoted by the town's Corporation and leading merchants. Early in the 18th century, to overcome the poor mooring facilities on the river and in the tidal inlet, known as the 'Pool', the Corporation ordered the construction of an enclosed wet dock. This, the first purpose-built commercial wet dock in the world, was built by Thomas Steers and opened in 1715. Later adapted to form part of the growing dock system, and then filled in and built over, the walls of the dock survive in part below ground. Tiny by later standards, the dock was, nevertheless, a significant investment for the Corporation, seeking to encourage

Fig 4 *St Nicholas's Church, George's Dock Basin and the warehouses on New Quay. This photograph of c 1880 gives some impression of the everyday scene on the quayside: a forest of masts can be seen in Prince's Dock to the left. [Local Illustrations Collection 326, Liverpool Record Office, Liverpool Libraries]*

Fig 5 *The Albert Dock and its warehouses, the work of Jesse Hartley, opened in 1846. [AA029235]*

merchants to use the port. Over the next century, the docks grew until, by 1810, they could be described as 'the most indubitable memorials of mercantile enterprize and transcendent utility' (Troughton 1810, 271). Later growth was even more spectacular, and ultimately the docks occupied an 11-kilometre frontage to the river. The greatest name associated with this huge endeavour is Jesse Hartley, Dock Engineer from 1824 to 1860, for it was he who designed and engineered the most notable facilities, those at Albert, Stanley and Wapping Docks, with their heroically scaled warehouses (Fig 5).

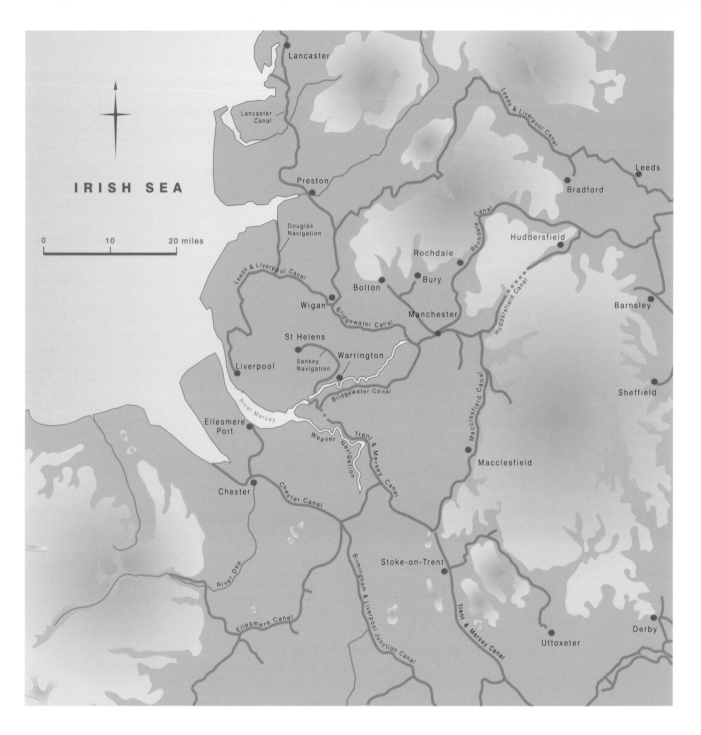

IRISH SEA

Lancaster

Lancaster
Canal

Preston

Douglas
Navigation

Leeds & Liverpool Canal

Leeds & Liverpool Canal

Leeds

Bradford

Huddersfield

Rochdale Canal

Rochdale

Bury

Bolton

Wigan

Bridgewater Canal

Manchester

Barnsley

St Helens

Warrington

Sankey
Navigation

Liverpool

Bridgewater Canal

Huddersfield Canal

Sheffield

River Mersey

Ellesmere
Port

Weaver Navigation

Trent & Mersey Canal

Macclesfield Canal

Chester

Chester Canal

Macclesfield

River Dee

Birmingham & Liverpool Junction Canal

Stoke-on-Trent

Ellesmere Canal

Trent & Mersey Canal

Uttoxeter

Derby

0   10   20 miles

Fig 6 Liverpool and its region, showing the pre-1850 navigation systems, which linked the port with a vast manufacturing and agricultural hinterland.

Liverpool was connected to its hinterland by an important network of waterways (Fig 6). Already in the late 17th century, the Mersey was made navigable as far upstream as Warrington, and, before the age of the railways, the Douglas, Weaver and Irwell rivers were improved to take water transport, and the Sankey, Bridgewater and Leeds & Liverpool canals were opened. In 1810 it was said that Liverpool's 'contiguity to navigable rivers; namely the Dee, the Weaver, and the Irwell; the numerous canals; and its spacious docks, so conveniently arranged for communication with each other and the river; its vicinity to Manchester, and its facility of intercourse with Birmingham and other distant manufacturing towns' made it the natural focus of trading activity for the manufacturing regions of the west midlands, Lancashire and Yorkshire (Troughton 1810, 101). The opening in 1830 of the Liverpool and Manchester Railway, at first successful mainly in carrying passengers, ushered in the railway age and with it the prospect of speedier bulk transport throughout a national network. The city's crucial role as a destination for imports and exports was seriously threatened only in 1894, when the opening of the Manchester Ship Canal offered the inland industrial region the option of bypassing the port that for more than a century had served its trading activities.

The immense volume of trade that passed through Liverpool transformed the town, turning it from little more than a village into England's second city. Its population rose from 5,000 in 1700 to 25,000 in 1760, to 77,000 in 1800 and to 311,000 in 1841, and the built-up area swallowed formerly outlying villages such as Everton and Walton. The character of the city was decidedly commercial: the Town Hall of 1749–54 provided an Exchange for merchants on its ground floor; banks, chambers, shipping companies and insurance houses proliferated to service the trading activities of the port; and the Custom House, rebuilt many times, presided over the collection of excise. The great wealth accumulated in the course of business found architectural expression in a wide range of buildings for the affluent merchants and the business community: the substantial houses of the extensive Georgian and Victorian suburbs, the clubs and the cultural and professional institutions demonstrate that Liverpool's elite lived in fine style.

Fig 7 'View of the Harbour of Leverpool',
E Rooker, 1770. [Local Illustrations Collection 294,
Liverpool Record Office, Liverpool Libraries]

The everyday aspects of trading life were very evident in the town and gave it a distinctive character, much remarked upon by commentators (Fig 7): in 1820, for example, it was observed (Anon 1820, 188–9) that

> The Old Dock, running eastwards into the town, presents the interesting spectacle of a number of ships, which, two centuries ago, would have been thought a complete navy, floating, in perfect security, in the very heart of a large town, mingling their lofty masts in the perspective of houses, churches, and other public buildings, and immediately surrounded with shops . . . victualling and drinking houses, and stores and erections for every mechanical operation connected with the naval department.

Inland from the later docks, industries and warehousing developed alongside housing for the labouring classes. The transformation brought to the area was remarked upon in the late 19th century by J A Picton (1875, II, 43), Liverpool's chronicler of the period, who wrote of the formerly genteel area of Love Lane that:

> The opening of the canal changed entirely the whole aspect of affairs. The zephyrs became redolent of coal-dust. Merchandise and traffic, with their sordid requirements, soon absorbed the pleasant nooks and corners. Fashion and comfort took their flight to more congenial regions, and the neighbourhood was left to the bustle of active industry . . . Love Lane is still a shady avenue, but it is with shadows of huge piles of warehouses and the viaduct of the railway.

Picton (an architect rather than an engineer, and one who even considered the Albert Dock 'a hideous pile of naked brickwork' and an 'incarnation of ugliness') introduces the warehouse to this story (1875, I, 570). Liverpool's growth from a port of modest size in the early 18th century to the hub of an imperial trading network in the early 20th is strikingly represented in the development of this building type.

CHAPTER 2

The Liverpool warehousing system

The number and extraordinary magnitude of the warehouses which meet the eye in almost every direction in the vicinity of the docks, are very interesting to a stranger. Their elevation, by which the number of these indispensable receptacles of merchandise is increased upon a small space of ground, their convenient situation upon the quays, and the facility with which goods are hoisted up to the highest stories, entitle them to peculiar notice. These, in connection with the docks, so admirably constructed for convenience and the despatch of business, constitute Liverpool one of the most convenient ports in the world, and have, no doubt, a great share of influence in its commercial prosperity.

Anon 1820, 183–4

One of the principal requirements for a trading city is adequate and secure storage for the goods that flow through it, both those awaiting export or onward sea transport and those destined for the home market. In a city such as Liverpool, which dealt to a large degree in commodities subject to excise duties, the government attempted to control the traffic of goods so as to calculate and levy duties. The interests of traders and regulators were not always identical, and over the course of two centuries there developed a dual system of warehousing, one part serving the private merchant, the other the occupiers of the Custom House.

The private warehouse

Long before the construction of the great dockside bonded stores, the private warehouse provided the exclusive means of handling merchandise, and it remained an essential part of the city's commercial infrastructure well into the 20th century. The range of types and designs of private warehouses will be considered in Chapter 3. Here it is important to understand something of their origin, function and distribution, and of the impact that they made upon the town.

We do not know when the first warehouses were built in Liverpool, but it is safe to assume that many were constructed once confidence had

been gained in the future of the port. Early views of Liverpool show that warehouses of a type similar to surviving examples formed part of the urban landscape from the mid-18th century (Fig 8). As the trade of the port expanded, so more and more warehouses were built, at first in the heart of the old town and in the streets around Steers' Old Dock, later closely following the expansion of the dock system to north and south.

The earliest warehouses were built by merchants, often adjacent to their houses or at the back of their plots. The relationship is revealed in an advertisement of 1760, which offered for let 'a large commodious house now tenanted by Mr Matthew Strong, merchant, containing four rooms on a floor, with a compting [counting] house; and a warehouse wherein may be laid 70 hogsheads [large casks] of sugar on a floor', and a survey plan of 1810 depicts such a property in Hanover Street (Picton 1875, II, 38) (Fig 9). Picton, recalling this early period of warehouse building, stated that in the Old Dock area 'almost every merchant had his counting

Fig 8 *The scene on the quayside at Steers' Old Dock in 1773: the Custom House flies the 'Public Office Jack', and in the middle distance are three warehouses. The close connection between the dock and the town is vividly illustrated in this view. [Reproduced from W Enfield*, A History of Liverpool (1773), *Liverpool Record Office, Liverpool Libraries]*

Fig 9 *A typical house and warehouse complex in Hanover Street, redrawn from a sale plan of 1810. [Redrawn from an archive plan from Liverpool Record Office, Liverpool Libraries]*

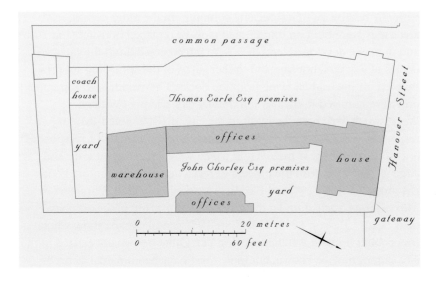

house at his back door. Henry Street [which runs behind one side of Duke Street] was lined with offices belonging to the merchants who resided in the houses in front'. There was, at that time, no stigma attached to 'living over the shop', and, in Picton's view, the nature of the trade brought few nuisances: he states (1875, II, 275–6) that

> the sugar, and molasses, and rum, with a few spices and fruit, which constituted the bulk of the returns, had nothing at all of a repulsive character in their aspect, and the hardware, clothing and provisions which were exported were equally harmless. The man-stealing process [that is, the slave trade which provided the third side of the merchants' Atlantic triangle] . . . the horrors of the baracoon [slave barracks], and of the middle passage, never obtruded themselves into the thoughts of the polite circles of Duke Street.

The growing scale of business, the fierce competition for land in the areas close to the docks and changing ideas on the proximity of places of residence and work soon led to the detachment of house and warehouse, and from the early 19th century free-standing warehouses, unassociated with any nearby dwelling, became common. In the older commercial areas they were built on unoccupied plots or replaced housing (Fig 10), and in newly developed land they were interspersed amid the factories, courts of workers' housing and timber yards of the sprawling suburbs that fed off the trade flowing from the docks. They made a strong impact on visitors unused to the life of a trading city: the poet William Wordsworth, writing after a visit to the city in 1819, noted that 'in respect of visual impression, nothing struck me so much at Liverpool as one of the streets near the river, in which were a number of lofty and large warehouses, with the process of receiving and discharging goods' (Moorman 1969, 229), and Elizabeth Gaskell's terrified characters in *Mary Barton* 'rushed under the great bales quivering in the air above their heads' (Easson 1993, 273). Late 19th-century maps show whole streets built up with warehouses (Fig 11). Quite how many existed in the city cannot now be known, but there must have been many hundreds.

At an unknown point in the 19th century, an important new development occurred with the emergence of the warehouse keeper as an agent serving the needs of the port. Where the merchant might own the goods that he stored, or at least hold them on behalf of an owner, the warehouse keeper seems mainly to have provided storage space for hire. Branckers, owners of one of the largest private warehouses in the city, may have provided storage space at their Great Howard Street warehouse from the 1840s, and in 1865 James Aspinall Brancker is recorded as warehouse keeper at this location. In 1851 sixteen warehouse keepers were listed in the Liverpool trade directory, most of them occupying office premises in the central commercial area and, presumably, owning warehouses in outlying parts close to the docks. The Liverpool Warehousing Co Ltd, established in 1895, came to own more than 400 warehouses, in Manchester as well as Liverpool, and in 1915 there were firms entitled 'The Liverpool Storage Co Ltd', 'The Liverpool Warehouse Construction Co Ltd' and 'The Liverpool and Manchester Cotton and Produce Storage Co Ltd' (Fig 12). The trade of the city had developed a long way from the stage when the typical business unit was that of a merchant operating from a small warehouse next to his house.

Fig 10 *The crowded commercial centre of Liverpool was full of warehouses in the early 19th century: two are visible here, on Mathew Street and Temple Court. [AA045283]*

Fig 11 *By the late 19th century, the area close to the docks was solidly built up with warehouses, housing and industrial premises. This fire insurance plan shows streets of warehouses, many used to store cotton. [Charles Goad Fire Insurance Plan, 1888, Vol I, Sheet 2, Liverpool Record Office, Liverpool Libraries]*

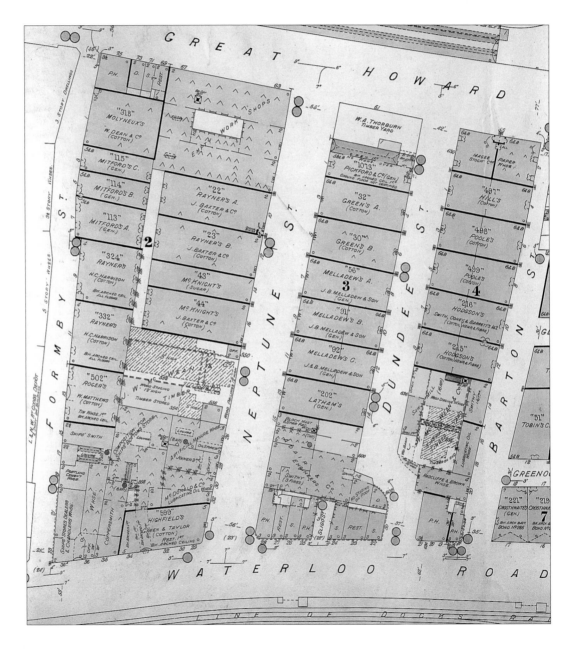

Fig 12 *Warehousing companies advertised their presence with bold signs: this warehouse is in Maddrell Street. [AA045284]*

Dock estate and bonded warehouses

Complementing the private warehouse in Liverpool was the provision of secure, regulated storage connected with the administration of excise duties on imported goods. At first, Customs officers were obliged to assess duties on the open quaysides before goods were taken away to private warehouses, very much as depicted in a view of the Old Dock made in 1773 (*see* Fig 8). Opportunities for evasion of duty were common, and as trade grew the potential loss of revenue to the government became unacceptably high. A model for secure dockside storage was first provided in Liverpool by Francis, 3rd Duke of Bridgewater, who in 1783 constructed a large stone warehouse, in what was known as Duke's Dock, a little to the south of the Old Dock. The provision of bonded storage, under crown locks, was introduced in Liverpool with the construction in 1795 of the first Tobacco Warehouse

Fig 13 *The King's Tobacco Warehouses of 1795,*
with a ten-storey warehouse in the background.
[From T Troughton, The History of Liverpool
(1810), Liverpool Record Office, Liverpool Libraries]

on the King's Dock (Fig 13). This heavily charged cargo was henceforth transferred immediately to the crown warehouse. The capacity for storage was extended in 1811 when a new and much bigger tobacco warehouse was built at the same dock; together the two warehouses could hold 30,000 hogsheads of leaf. The security of crown stores worked not only to the excise man's advantage, for the merchants too benefited: if they re-exported the goods, no duty was payable, and payments on goods destined for the home market were deferred until they were removed from the warehouse.

Bonded storage found wider application after 1805, when the provisions of the 1803 Warehousing Act, at first limited to London, were extended to Liverpool and other ports. In London the Act was a response to the construction of secure warehousing around new enclosed docks at the West India and London Docks of 1800–5. But in Liverpool nothing comparable to the West India Docks was built for nearly half a century. Instead, the Act led to the simple upgrading of the sometimes-leaky private warehouses in the town to meet certain conditions for secure bonded storage and to the appointment of lockers to keep these buildings under crown locks. Conversion of existing warehouses was relatively inexpensive, and despite the loss of a degree of independent action, many merchants clearly considered conformity to be in their interests, for by 1820 there were 164 bonded warehouses in the town.

Only with the opening of Jesse Hartley's Albert Dock in 1846 was London's enclosed warehouse-dock system, fully developed at St Katherine Docks in the 1820s, introduced to Liverpool. At Albert, the great warehouses that so offended Picton were an integral part of the scheme: ships in the dock unloaded directly on to a secure quay where duty could be assessed, and goods were then taken into the warehouses for storage without the payment of dues (Fig 14). Albert at first mainly handled North American and Far Eastern trade, and the warehouses provided bonded storage for goods such as silks, cotton, tea, sugar, rice, wool and spices, in quantities that earlier warehouses had never approached: the stacks around the dock could hold approximately 250,000 tonnes of goods. The immense size of the warehouses reflects

Fig 14 *The Albert Dock and warehouses, opened in 1846, provided a secure environment for the unloading and storage of valuable goods. The contrast with the earlier arrangement around the Old Dock (see Fig 8) is clear. [AA029119]*

Fig 15 *The Tobacco Warehouse in Stanley Dock. Built in the years 1897–1901 to designs by Anthony George Lyster, the fourteen-storey warehouse has hydraulic lifts and hoists. [AA045290]*

the volume of trade and the need for huge quantities of long-term storage space; cotton, for example, was stockpiled here awaiting favourable market conditions.

The construction of Albert Dock was followed by the addition of further docks and warehouses on the same principle: Stanley Dock was opened in 1848 and Wapping Dock in 1855, and large warehouses, similar to those at Albert Dock, were built around them. As well as large, multi-storeyed warehouses, transit sheds were also constructed on the quayside, but, as the name suggests, they were intended only for short-term storage while goods were checked, weighed and sorted. Some later dock or dock-area warehouses were built for specific purposes. A huge grain warehouse, a pioneer in the loose handling of this commodity, was built from 1866 to 1868 at East Waterloo Dock (*see* Fig 42), and the Colonial Warehouse in Love Lane (demolished) stored colonial wool imports. But the greatest warehouse of all in terms of scale was the Tobacco Warehouse built within Stanley Dock in the years 1897–1901 (Fig 15). Fourteen storeys high (including the vaults), using steel beams and iron columns, and towering over Hartley's earlier buildings, this was said to be the largest warehouse in the world. If any single building expresses Liverpool's role in a great trading network, this is it.

CHAPTER 3

The design and construction of warehouses

The warehouse is a simple building type with a limited range of design considerations. There is little evidence in surviving warehouses for the processing of goods, and overwhelmingly the dominant purpose of the type was the storage of commodities, which had to be kept in good condition, dry, and secure from pests, theft and fire. The design of warehouses, therefore, has a number of determinants. The availability of land influenced the 'footprint' of the building and therefore its overall form, and the nature of the packaging, the weight of loads and the means of lifting goods externally and internally dictated aspects such as floor heights, floor construction and the size of openings. The need for security and the containment of fire led to design changes in the 19th century, but always the form of warehouses reflected sober risk assessment and the search for the optimum balance between, on the one hand, the use of the building and, on the other, cost and quality of construction.

Early warehouses

The form of the most common warehouse type was established by at least as early as the mid-18th century, although no buildings survive from that date. Early views show that modestly sized, multi-storeyed warehouses formed part of street scenes in the old town centre. They occupied narrow plots, perhaps established hundreds of years earlier, and, unable to spread out to the sides and rear, succeeded in providing extensive storage space by stacking floors one on top of the other. Forced upwards rather than outwards by the size of their plots and the cost of land in the centre of the town, the warehouses required a means of lifting goods to the upper floors, and so a hoist, at this date manually powered, was set in the roof space, hauling sacks, casks and other loads up the face of the building to where they could be stored.

This type of warehouse was common in English trading towns in the 18th century, and some survive in ports such as Lancaster, Whitehaven and Hull. The earliest Liverpool warehouses that remain date from the late 18th century and are concentrated close to the earliest docks, where most of the wealthy merchants lived. Here are found a number of examples of the combined house and warehouse noted by Picton

(and found also in Whitehaven and Hull). The grandest was built by the
wealthy merchant and banker Thomas Parr on Colquitt Street, just off
Duke Street (Fig 16). Built in the 1790s, the fine mansion has a five-bay,
three-storeyed block flanked by pavilions, and behind this domestic
accommodation, on Parr Street, is a handsome, tall warehouse. In its size
and with its fine stone details around windows, pediment and gables, the
warehouse reflects the standing of the builder and the quality of his
house. Other large houses associated with warehouses are 139 Dale
Street and 9 York Street; at the latter the warehouse forms a wing

Fig 16 *One of the wealthiest Liverpool merchants and
bankers, Thomas Parr, built his warehouse immediately
behind his town house on Colquitt Street. [AA041183]*

Fig 17 *The warehouse at 42 Fleet Street forms a wing to a short terrace of houses. [AA045285]*

attached to the rear of the five-bay town house. Much smaller is the three-storeyed warehouse at 42 Fleet Street, built as a wing to a short terrace of houses on Slater Street (Fig 17). The scale of business operations and the close relationship between trade and domestic life in the late 18th century are vividly illustrated in these buildings: it is easy to imagine cotton or rum being checked into the warehouse under the watchful eye of the merchant, who had perhaps supervised transport from the nearby public quay, and we can understand how the proximity of the house provided a degree of security against theft.

The early warehouses are of simple form. They vary in height from the three-storey buildings on College Lane (Fig 18) to the six storeys of 46 Henry Street (Fig 19a–d) and share many common features. They are built of brick, attractive in colour and texture, although not intended for decorative effect. All the design features of the building – loading doors, pedestrian access, stair, hoist – are on or just behind the street elevation; behind this is simply space for storage. The central bay on the front wall is occupied by a tier of loading doors, set just behind the wall face, and over the loading doors there projects a timber hoist beam. The raised ground floor made it easier to move goods directly to and from carts. The position of the stair is indicated by the tier of small oval windows at one end of the elevation: designed to admit light, their size

a

b

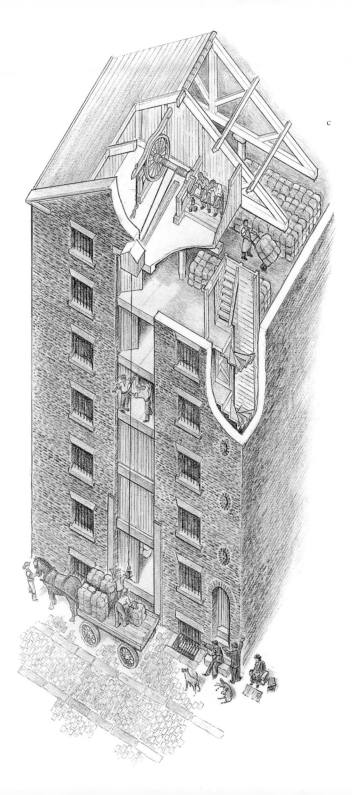

Fig 18 *(opposite, bottom left) A pair of late 18th-century warehouses on College Lane: the timber doors and hoist beams and the small oval windows lighting the stairs are typical of the period. [AA045335]*

Fig 19 *46 Henry Street:*

(a) detail of the stair window [AA045277];

(b) elevation [AA045275];

(c) goods being hoisted into one of the upper floors; and

(d) warehousemen grappling with a bale to pull it into the warehouse.

27

and the iron grilles prevented the pilferage of goods. Pedestrian doors, again narrow to discourage theft, give access to the base of the stair.

Internally, nothing in the scale of most warehouses challenged the building technology of the age. In an era when much larger canal warehouses, military storehouses and mills were being constructed, these modest buildings represented an everyday constructional exercise for the jobbing builder. They had timber floors of substantial joists laid on heavy, square-section beams, usually supported by timber stanchions (Fig 20). The stair was commonly of timber, with narrow treads rising around a newel (Fig 21). Roof trusses were of timber: where spans were modest, king-post trusses could be used, but in wider buildings queen-strut and collar trusses provided the necessary breadth.

Because warehouses were commonly hemmed in on both sides by other buildings, natural light was in short supply: many warehouses had windows only in the front elevation and in some cases at the back as well. Oil lamps, a considerable fire hazard, were commonly used to provide more light. Ample lighting was not as critical in a storage warehouse as it was in, say, a Manchester packing warehouse or a textile mill, since for most of the time goods simply sat awaiting their next move: the light and clatter of a mill can be contrasted with the usual gloom and tomb-like silence of the warehouse (Fig 22). Conformity to the regulations governing bonded storage led to a reduction in natural lighting, for at warehouses like 38 Henry Street the original windows, of generous size, were blocked to incorporate a much more secure small opening (Fig 23).

If the six-storey warehouse at 46 Henry Street appears large alongside many others of the same period, it was dwarfed by a few warehouses of prodigious size, higher than anything built in Liverpool until the construction of the Tobacco Warehouse at Stanley Dock in 1900. The first Goree Warehouses (their name was derived from the notorious slave-trading island off Senegal), built beside George's Dock by the Corporation in 1793 (but used by merchants as private warehouses), were said to have been in part of thirteen storeys, and in the same year one observer noted that 'on the sides of the docks are warehouses of uncommon size and strength, far surpassing in those respects the warehouses of London. To their different floors, often ten or

Fig 20 *(opposite, top) The loading bay on the fourth floor of 46 Henry Street: the view shows the timber floor and timber prop. The rope harnesses hanging from the beam secured the warehousemen as they pulled goods into the building. [AA045279]*

Fig 21 *(opposite, bottom) The timber stair at 46 Henry Street. [AA045276]*

Fig 22 *(above, left) The gloomy interior of 46 Henry Street: natural light would be supplemented by the light of oil lamps. [AA045280]*

Fig 23 *(above, right) A large window blocked to provide a small shuttered opening in the warehouse at 38 Henry Street: this may have resulted from the need to conform to the requirements for bonded storage. [AA045291]*

eleven in number, goods are carried up with great facility' (Aikin 1795, 355). The great height of these warehouses, which must have made the movement of goods extremely laborious, indicates the value of this prime location, close to the early docks, and a wish to provide as much storage space as the confined site would allow. The impression made by these mammoth structures is especially understandable when a search for contemporary comparisons is made: London, our observer states, cannot match these buildings (although we know that nine-storey warehouses were built there in the 18th century), and it is quite possible that, apart from churches, the Liverpool warehouses were, when built, the tallest structures in the country.

The 19th-century warehouse

The great period of warehouse construction was the 19th century, when the success of the port depended on storage facilities keeping pace with the phenomenal growth of the city's trade and with the changing needs of its merchants, shippers and brokers. Different types of warehouse and new structural forms developed in this period, but there was also a strong element of continuity, for still at the end of the century warehouses were being built that were recognisable as the descendants of their 18th-century predecessors.

Many of the multi-storeyed warehouses of the 19th century had the same small footprint as their earlier counterparts, and like them rose tall – often to six or eight storeys – to provide a reasonable amount of storage space. The grouping of warehouse units within a single large building, as at the post-fire Goree Warehouses (Fig 24), became more common: streets became canyons, their sides punctuated with a regular rhythm of loading door and window openings (Fig 25). The provision of multiple units suggests that warehouse ownership was now seen very firmly as a profitable business: the owner might not be directly involved in trade, but could draw rents from the businesses that occupied his building.

Fig 24 *The Goree Warehouses as rebuilt after the fire of 1802: in the background can be seen a much taller warehouse of eleven storeys. [From T Troughton,* The History of Liverpool *(1810), Liverpool Record Office, Liverpool Libraries]*

Fig 25 *A multiple-unit warehouse on Parliament Street, built in the late 19th century, probably by the Liverpool Warehouse Construction Company Ltd. [AA045293]*

Fig 26 *One of many destructive warehouse fires: New Quay burns down in 1833. [Local Illustrations Collection 82, Liverpool Record Office, Liverpool Libraries]*

One common characteristic of the 18th-century warehouse – its proximity to the merchant's house – was slowly eroded in the 19th century. Social and cultural reasons led the merchant to separate his home from work and to move his place of residence away from the Old Dock area, where commerce and industry now provided the dominant tone. Further from the heart of the town, behind the growing dock estate, the many new warehouses looked not to the merchant's house but to his office in the centre of the city, where all the business was transacted. The warehouse areas thus became places exclusively where goods were stored: deals were done elsewhere.

The overall form of the multi-storeyed warehouses may have altered little over the course of the 19th century, but there were, nonetheless, considerable changes in construction. The most significant impetus behind these changes concerned the fear of fire (Fig 26). The century was ushered in with the great conflagration of 1802, which consumed the massive Goree Warehouses, destroying the buildings and their contents, threatening neighbouring buildings and shipping in the adjacent dock, and causing losses valued at more than £300,000, a vast sum at the time. In a single year, 1842, there were 140 warehouse fires: one, the Formby Street fire, destroyed nine warehouses and property to the value of over £500,000. The risk of fire stemmed principally from the use of naked flames for lighting: a lamp, once inadvertently toppled, could quickly set alight dry stored goods, and the blaze could then spread rapidly throughout the building. In the days of rudimentary fire fighting, the job was to confine the fire to a single warehouse.

The prevention and containment of fire, therefore, were of vital interest to all parties – the Corporation, warehouse, shipping and property owners, and insurance companies. As a result, a number of local Building Acts (1825, 1835, 1842 and 1843) were passed to regulate the design of warehouses and the subject of better warehouse building was discussed in the literature of the time. No attempt was made to enforce the use of fireproof construction such as had been developed for textile mills in the late 18th century and become commonplace by the mid-19th century, for it was accepted that the economics of warehousing made this inappropriate in most cases. Instead, the Acts stipulated the use of simple, sensible structural features to make warehouses less prone to failure and to limit the consequences of collapse. External and internal walls and floor and roof timbers were to be of a certain thickness, and internal dividing walls were to have metal doors in an attempt to confine fire to a single compartment. The provision of a fireproof stair bay, again with metal doors, inhibited the spread of fire from floor to floor, as well, of course, as providing a safe means of exit for warehouse workers. Cast-iron columns were stipulated for use on the ground floor, and overall height restrictions, varying according to the width of the street, were introduced. The spread of flames from building to building was to be inhibited by the use of parapet and party walls rising above the roof line, and external features – gutters, hoist beams, lean-to structures, doors and windows – were to be of non-combustible materials. From 1843, warehouses were registered and graded according to their degree of conformity to the Building Acts; the safest, enjoying lower insurance

a

Fig 27 *15 Duke Street, built in 1864.*

(a) *The elevation shows the effect of the Building Acts in encouraging the use of fireproof features in the openings. [AA045294]*

(b) *The floors of this warehouse are of timber construction. [AA98/02366]*

(c) *The stair is of cast iron and is contained within a brick stair compartment entered through a sheet-iron door. [AA98/02367]*

(d) *The warehouse hoist survives in the 'jigger loft'. [AA98/02368]*

b

c

d

premiums, were the fully fireproof warehouses, but there were four other grades, acknowledging that non-fireproof buildings would continue to be constructed.

Together the Building Acts and the requirements of bonded storage changed the construction of warehouses. One building may be taken to illustrate the differences between the mid-19th-century warehouse and its 18th-century predecessor. The warehouse at 15 Duke Street was built in 1864, and, while not entirely typical of its period, it shows many of the improvements of the age. It is of four storeys above a basement, but looks taller because the roof rises at the front to provide a 'jigger loft' containing the hoists (Fig 27a–d). It has the conventional narrow frontage to the street, but within this elevation it provides two tiers of loading doors. As in earlier warehouses, the ground floor is raised above street level to facilitate the movement of goods from carts: virtually all private warehouses depended solely on road transport. Fire containment and security are evident in a number of external and internal features. Iron was used in place of timber in and around the openings on the street elevation – the doors and floor ends in the loading bays, the narrow pedestrian door set in a cast-iron frame, the hoist beams, with the date 1864, and the shutters to the narrow barred windows. Internally, safe exit from the building was assisted by the use of a cast-iron spiral stair within a brick stair compartment. Too confined to permit the movement of goods, the stair communicated with each floor and even the 'jigger loft' – after all, the hoist man had the furthest to go to get out of a blazing warehouse – through doorways with cast-iron frames and sheet-iron doors.

Despite all these improvements, the building is otherwise structurally similar to earlier warehouses: it uses heavy softwood timbers in its roof trusses and floors (the latter propped by cast-iron columns as stipulated by the Building Acts). An internal timber structure was the norm in multi-storeyed warehouses throughout the 19th century, and clearly it was regarded that this, rather than an over-specified fireproof structure, was what the economics of the business could sustain.

We know little about the conditions of work and of the workforce in the typical private warehouse. Warehouse work was a male occupation, but not necessarily very steady in its nature, for casual, day labour may have been used to take on men only when needed. It is likely that small numbers were employed, for although packages could be heavy, only one could be on the move at any one time in a warehouse with a single tier of loading doors. Early photographs reveal that there were periods of intense activity, as shipments arrived or left the warehouse. Some men were required to handle goods on a cart outside; others transferred goods into or out of one of the floors of the building; and one or more men operated the manually powered hoist in the hoist loft. The work of the warehouse was probably supervised by a foreman, but the buildings show no evidence for the provision of offices for paperwork. Also absent is any sanitation, which suggests that the workforce may not have been permanently based at the warehouse, but instead moved around between the dock, the town-centre offices and the warehouse, spending time at the last only when there were goods to move.

The operation of manual hoists was regarded as something of a problem. It was observed in 1869 (Boult 1869, 86–7) that

> in lofty warehouses, it is sometimes necessary to have relays of men, and then six or eight men may be found on a hot summer's day, sweltering in the jigger loft close to the hot slates, and without any appreciable ventilation. Now, of course, when men of the class usually employed are so far removed from observation; there is great probability, not to say certainty, that one or more will smoke or drink; as smoking and drinking are gregarious habits, it is very likely that all, or almost all, will offend in this way, any prohibition in the Act of Parliament to the contrary notwithstanding.

The consequent risk of fire and injury was taken seriously, and alternatives to the manual hoist were sought. There was some use of steam and gas engines and of hoists worked by compressed air, but hydraulic power, widely used in the dock estate, appears only rarely to have assisted work in the smaller warehouses, because in the middle decades of the century the supply of power proved unreliable. Only late in the 19th century did an extensive network providing a reliable supply develop across the city.

Fireproof, low-rise and combined-use warehouses

Although most 19th-century warehouses were multi-storeyed and of conventional construction, a substantial number adopted different designs. Some of these were built to be fireproof; others displayed a different overall form; and still others combined warehousing with other types of accommodation – shops and offices – to create a new mixed-use building type.

The best-known fireproof warehouses are those built by Jesse Hartley on the Dock Estate. The warehouses around Albert Dock, Stanley Dock and Wapping Dock were executed on a Herculean scale for bonded storage, at last providing the port of Liverpool with facilities to match those of the London docks. The internal structure of these warehouses has a massive solidity: graceful brick vaults spring from

Fig 28 *The Albert Dock warehouses have brick-vaulted ceilings, visible here in the quayside arcade. [AA030736]*

Fig 29 *This warehouse at 68 Waterloo Road, at the junction with Vulcan Street, was probably built in the mid-1840s as a fireproof building. [AA045126]*

substantial cast-iron beams, supported at intervals by iron columns (Fig 28). The heaviness of this structure contrasts, in the Albert Dock warehouses, with that of the roof, which has light, almost bow-profile wrought-iron trusses supporting a roof covering of iron sheets, the last galvanised to protect against corrosion.

The construction of Hartley's great dock warehouses was determined by unique criteria. The requirement was for secure bonded storage on a scale that dwarfed all private warehousing, and the finance was provided by the Corporation and Dock Trustees. The projects were not, therefore, governed solely by commercial considerations. These conditions did not apply outside the Dock Estate, but nevertheless for some warehouse builders fireproof construction, albeit on a more modest scale, was the preferred option. The Formby Street fire of 1842 provided a lesson: just one warehouse, significantly of fireproof construction, withstood the conflagration. Probably shortly thereafter, a fireproof warehouse was built on Waterloo Road (Fig 29), and this was quickly followed by the construction of P W Brancker's enormous Clarence Warehouses on Great Howard Street (Fig 30a–h). In the course of construction in 1844 (and therefore almost exactly contemporary with the Albert Dock warehouses), this block was of conventional plan and form but entirely fireproof in construction, with brick-arched floors and a roof of cast and wrought iron. It appears to have been built in phases and was probably designed to provide multiple units that might be let separately. Its earliest recorded use is indicated by the Ordnance Survey map of 1848, which shows it as a corn store. Although valuable and combustible, corn did not rival some other goods in either risk or value, but Brancker was clearly concerned to provide the safest environment that contemporary technology could devise. The scale and construction of the building together set it apart from all other surviving private warehouses of the period.

Very much at the same time as Brancker was building Clarence Warehouses, a markedly different form of warehouse was appearing in the areas behind the new docks to north and south of the city centre. This was the 'low-rise' warehouse, sometimes with one, sometimes with

a

b

c

d

e

Fig 30 *Clarence Warehouses, 177 Great Howard Street. This very large multiple-unit warehouse was built in fireproof form in the mid-1840s, probably by the building firm A H Holme.*

(a) The elevation to Dickson Street has ten loading bays. [AA045316]

(b) The warehouse's features include sheet-iron doors and window shutters and cast-iron window sills and lintels. [AA045317]

(c) The ceilings have brick vaults and tile floors. [AA045324]

(d) The staircases are fully fireproof. [AA045327]

(e) Openings in party walls have double-leaf sheet-iron doors. [AA045323]

Fig 30 *continued*

(f) *The roof structure uses triangulated trusses of cast and wrought iron. [AA045326]*

(g) *Parapet walls rise above the roof to prevent the spread of fire from unit to unit. [AA045322]*

(h) *The section shows the fireproof construction.*

h

4

3

2

1

G

B

0   10 metres

0   30 feet

Fig 31 *A low-rise warehouse at 8 Grundy Street: note how the loading bays have doors only on the raised ground floor.* [AA045299]

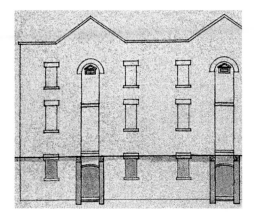
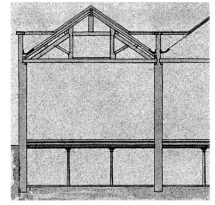
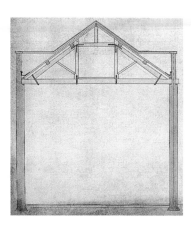

Fig 32a *Elevation and sections of a warehouse on Sefton Street, designed by William Culshaw, 1845: the sections show clear floor heights of 21 feet and 28 feet (6.4 and 8.5 metres). [Sections reproduced with the consent of Edmund Kirby & Sons from the Culshaw Collection, Lancashire Record Office (DDX 162)]*

Fig 32b *Very lofty storage areas were provided at the low-rise warehouse at 8–10 Glegg Street. [AA045286]*

two floors over a basement (Fig 31). It is likely that land in these outlying commercial districts was cheaper than in the city centre, and that open ground could be developed by dividing it up into generous plots unconstrained by existing buildings and complex ownership patterns. Larger plots, therefore, could be afforded, and, although the option was not universally adopted, many warehouse developers chose to build broad and low rather than tall and narrow, probably for the advantages in goods handling that the low-rise warehouse offered. Many of these warehouses were of fireproof construction. Some, at least, had a further distinguishing feature, that is, the provision of much greater ceiling heights in one or more of their floors than is found in multi-storeyed warehouses. A single-storey warehouse of 1845 in Sefton Street had headroom rising to 28 feet (8.5 metres); at Glegg Street a surviving two-storeyed warehouse has a ground floor rising to over 6 metres (Fig 32a–b); and fireproof warehouses in Birchall Street have a ground-floor height of 4.5 metres (Fig 33a–d). These buildings could, therefore, store goods in much loftier stacks, and in the Birchall Street warehouses cast-iron hooks let into the brick vaults were probably used for lifting gear to raise loads above normal unassisted storage heights. It is probable that the low-rise warehouse proved suited to particular trades: it might, for example, have been relatively easy to stack cotton bales to greater heights than could be managed with some other commodities. Both single-storeyed and two-storeyed versions of the low-rise warehouse were built before 1850, and continued to be built into the early 20th century, when the use of light angle-iron roof trusses permitted wide unobstructed storage areas on the upper floor (Fig 34).

a

b

c

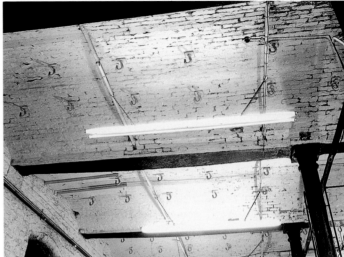

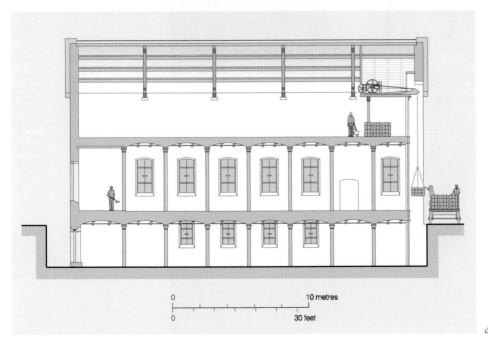

Fig 33 *Warehouses at 2–4 Birchall Street.*

(a) *These late 19th-century warehouses are of low-rise form, with two storeys over a basement. [AA045295]*

(b) *Fireproof construction is used internally over the lofty ground floor. [AA045296]*

(c) *Hooks in the ground-floor ceiling vaults were probably used to assist lifting heavy loads. [AA045297]*

(d) *The section shows the height of the ground floor.*

d

Fig 34 *62–4 Kitchen Street, built in the early 20th century, has a wide span permitted by the use of light angle-iron roof trusses. [AA045301]*

Fig 35 *(opposite page) Rigby's Buildings, Dale Street.*

(a) *The Victorian façade hides a small courtyard behind. [AA029162]*

(b) *An earlier warehouse – now converted into flats – is found along one side. [AA045302]*

a

b

A new type of mixed-use building was developed in the early and mid-19th century. The centre of the city retains a number of stylish warehouses of this period, showing that the narrow streets here must have been cluttered with goods moving to and from the docks at this time (Fig 35a–b). In the course of the century, however, the historic centre was largely rebuilt: existing streets were widened and new streets were laid out, lined with large, impressive commercial buildings – offices, hotels, banks and so on. But warehousing remained important even in the heart of the Victorian commercial district, for in the streets and lanes leading off the principal routes – Dale Street and Victoria Street – are to be found the familiar features of warehouse architecture.

These features are found both in largely conventional warehouses, such as are found in Cheapside (Fig 36), and, more significantly, in buildings in which warehousing was just one component. An early example is found in Sweeting Street: here, Barned's Buildings, of the 1830s, provides a dignified classical range of offices set above a warehouse basement (Fig 37). A later and grander example of the same mixed use is The Albany, Old Hall Street, designed by J K Colling and built in 1856. Anything less like a Liverpool warehouse is difficult to imagine, for it is an ornate Renaissance palace, the style providing a link between the city's business community and the merchant princes of Venice and Lombardy (Fig 38a–c). Above street level, the building provided suites of offices, once populated by an army of clerks in dozens of different firms. But the basement provides storage space, and teagles (cast-iron cranes) on the long side walls enabled goods to be moved from the street to the lower level. The amount of storage space is much smaller than the amount of office space, and it is likely that the basement either held samples, perhaps of cotton, or operated entirely independently of the businesses on the upper floors. If the latter, the provision of warehousing in the basement offered the speculator the prospect of additional income for parts of the building that could not provide good office space. Subterranean Liverpool was a warren of storage vaults.

In many other mixed-use buildings, the functional distinction is not between upper and lower levels but between front and rear: instead of

Fig 36 *27 Cheapside: note the use of fireproof doors, large windows with cast-iron sills and lintels, and decorative polychrome brickwork.* [AA045303]

Fig 37 *(opposite page) Barned's Buildings, Sweeting Street. The handsome Classical office building has a storage basement, served by the cast-iron cranes attached to the wall. External access to the basement has now been blocked.* [AA045305]

a

b

Fig 38 *The Albany, Old Hall Street, built in 1856.*

(a) The fine office façade, illustrated in a contemporary watercolour, disguises the storage use of the basement. [Herdman Collection Index 496, Liverpool Record Office, Liverpool Libraries]

(b) The side elevation has cranes that were used to move goods to and from the basement. [AA041224]

(c) The reconstruction drawing shows how the warehousing was segregated from the office accommodation on the upper floors.

c

Fig 39a *(left) Westminster Chambers, Dale Street, 1879–80, designed by Robert Owens for David Roberts. The Gothic style of the office elevation contrasts with the plain warehouse elevation on Preston Street. [AA045306]*

Fig 39b *(below) Westminster Chambers, Dale Street. The plan shows that there was no doorway connection between the two parts of the building.*

being hidden below street level, warehousing was located behind the less conspicuous elevations of buildings. A good example is Westminster Chambers, built in 1879–80. The façades to Dale Street and Crosshall Street are of sandstone and are dressed up in an ornate Gothic style: the windows in the elevations light two principal floors of offices above a row of shops. But, turning the corner into Preston Street, a minor backstreet, stone gives way to pale brick and functionalism replaces ornament, for on this front the building provided warehouses, with four tiers of loading doors (Fig 39a–b). The same is encountered in Victoria Street, where a long line of office buildings – Crown Buildings,

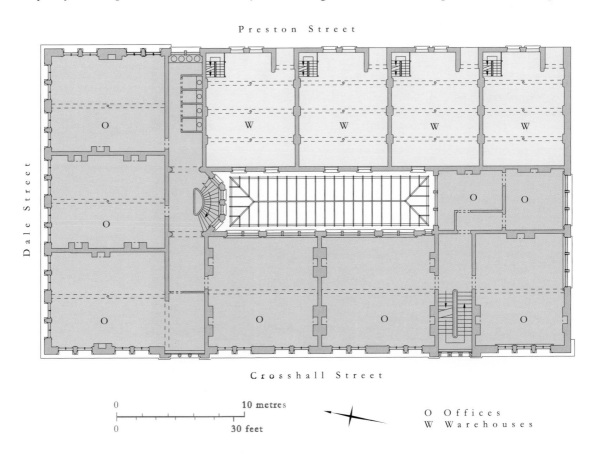

Preston Street

Dale Street

Crosshall Street

| 0 | | 10 metres |
| 0 | | 30 feet |

O Offices
W Warehouses

Fig 40a *The Crown, Jerome, Carlisle and Abbey Buildings on Victoria Street all date from the mid-1880s. [AA040555]*

Fig 40b *Crown, Jerome, Carlisle and Abbey Buildings, Victoria Street. At the rear, the range provides warehouses. [AA045309]*

Fig 41 *Shared stairways, with pale blue brickwork and iron balusters, give access to the offices in Jerome Buildings, Victoria Street. [AA045308]*

Jerome Buildings, Carlisle Buildings and Abbey Buildings, all of the mid-1880s and all with stylish street frontages – betray their dual function in their rear elevation, where, towering over a narrow street, is a sheer wall punctured by tiers of loading doors (Fig 40a–b). Many of these city-centre warehouses have much better lighting than their more remote cousins, with much larger windows.

These buildings, and many others like them, were probably designed to be used flexibly. They could be rented in their entirety by a large company, or occupied by a number of companies renting out accommodation – perhaps a whole floor or part of a floor – to suit their needs. Some companies might require offices and a warehouse, some one and some the other. Shared staircases give access to the office areas on each floor (Fig 41) and, in some buildings at least, the warehouse parts could function entirely separately. The accommodation would be ideal for trades such as that of a cotton broker, wishing to conduct a business from prestigious offices but to have on hand, in an adjoining warehouse, a good range of samples. An illustration of how such structures were used is provided by the row on Victoria Street: in 1888 Crown Buildings housed a provision merchant, two clock manufacturers, a corn and flour dealer, a hardware merchant, an engineer and a 'horse nail' company, and Abbey Buildings contained a leather factor, a boot manufacturer, and a glass, lead, oil and colour merchant. It is quite clear that even in the late 19th century, property developers were keenly aware that the commercial life of the city centre depended on proximity between business accommodation and warehousing.

CHAPTER 4

Postscript: the decline of the Liverpool warehouse

As long as trade patterns and the means of moving and storing goods remained largely unchanged, Liverpool's warehouses performed an essential role in the economic life of the city. But forces beyond the city's control began, in the 20th century, to reduce their usefulness and to deplete the building stock. The collapse of the region's manufacturing economy in the middle decades of the century – particularly the loss of the cotton industry – reduced the flow of goods – both imports and exports – that for a century or more had sustained the life of the port. War, too, took its toll on warehouses, the blitz of 1941 razing many to the ground, and post-war reconstruction saw the demolition of many more.

The ways in which goods were moved around and packaged affected the nature of storage facilities. The movement of some bulk items like grain, which had been contained in sacks that a single man could carry, was mechanised so that the loose cargo could be transferred by elevators and conveyors for storage in hoppers. This change had begun in the 19th century, for the Waterloo Corn Warehouse of 1866–8 had been the first in the world to introduce fully mechanised working (Fig 42). The mid-20th-century sugar silo built by Tate and Lyle behind the northern docks

Fig 42 *(right) The surviving wing of the Waterloo Corn Warehouse, designed by G F Lyster and built in the years 1866–8 to provide fully mechanised movement of grain. [AA029293]*

developed the handling of bulk cargoes (Fig 43a–b), and the later storage tanks in the same area demonstrate how bulk liquids are handled in the modern age, a far cry from the casks and barrels of the 19th century (Fig 44). The introduction of container transport further reduced the handling of goods, and the development of the container port to the north effectively left the old docks, and the warehouses that had served them, isolated from the flow of traffic (Fig 45).

For less bulky commodities, the revolution in handling has been no less far-reaching. For these goods, the fork-lift truck has replaced muscle power, and this has had two consequences for warehousing. First, the fork-lift truck is more safely operated at ground level in unobstructed spaces rather than on the cluttered upper floors of a multi-storeyed warehouse. And, second, the vertical reach of the fork-lift truck is far greater than that possible by muscle power. Especially when aided by packing on pallets, goods of great weight can be stacked to much greater heights. Once this became possible, the advantages of ground-level storage became obvious, and the unsuitability of all but the low-rise warehouses for modern storage needs was plain to see. The future of most historic warehouses, therefore, depends upon finding new uses.

Fig 43a *(above, left) Tate and Lyle's Sugar Silo, 173 Regent Road, built 1955–7. The massive concrete arches provide an immense internal storage space.* [AA045127]

Fig 43b *(above, right) This interior view of Tate and Lyle's Sugar Silo shows the conveyer system on the roof of the building.* [BB92/8803]

Fig 44 *Modern bulk storage in the docks: the lorries on Regent Road show how bulk materials are now transported. [AA045266]*

Fig 45 *The container port: giant cranes lift the containers from ships to stacks on the quayside, and then on to lorries for onward transport. The port lies to the north of the old dock area. [Reproduced with permission of The Mersey Docks and Harbour Company; DP002421]*

CHAPTER 5

The conservation of Liverpool's warehouses

Liverpool's warehouses, great and small, are the most powerful symbols of its maritime character and they provide much of the support for the bid for World Heritage Site status, contributing a strong commercial element to the urban landscape and exemplifying the city's tradition of technological and architectural innovation. In recent decades, our view of their significance has been radically changed. Instead of being seen as evidence of economic decline, the city's warehouses are now recognised as crucial assets of an historic landscape that is undergoing dynamic regeneration. But this renewed appreciation of warehouses needs to be translated into positive action if they are to remain as relevant to the future as they were to the past. Can these buildings be adapted to new uses, keeping pace with the creative forces that are re-shaping areas where the storage and transport of goods was once the dominant influence? If adaptive reuse is possible, can a workable balance between creative change and sensitive conservation be achieved?

The argument for retention and reuse rests on the widely held appreciation of the special character that warehouses give to Liverpool's historic environment. Perhaps in no other English city is such a variety of warehousing encountered: on the waterfront are the great dock warehouses, a magnet for visitors to the city; at every turn in the commercial centre one sees the familiar loading bays with their metal doors and hoists; and in some parts of the outlying areas, well away from the waterfront, singly or in groups, warehouses remind us of how deeply Liverpool's trading history is embedded in the fabric of the city. This distinctiveness is important, for in an age of increasing blandness it provides a powerful sense of place, satisfying to both residents and visitors. Loss of this distinctiveness would seriously weaken our connection with the past.

Much of this historic resource has already been lost. Of the hundreds of warehouses that existed at the beginning of the 20th century, perhaps only 150 remain today. Many of the surviving warehouses are in poor condition: the outstanding group around the Stanley Dock, including two warehouses of 1852–5 by Hartley and the immense Tobacco Warehouse, completed in 1901, remains one of the most severe conservation issues in the city. Just at the moment when the

Fig 46 *The office and warehouse at 12 Hanover Street, listed grade II. Built in 1889, it had offices on the main frontages and warehouses to the rear. Occupied in 1905 by a provision merchant, today it provides modern office accommodation. [AA026215]*

city's historic character is being recognised as internationally significant, it is more important than ever to manage this irreplaceable stock of buildings so that it can be enjoyed by this and future generations.

We can begin this process by protecting the best of what survives, and many warehouses are now listed buildings (Fig 46), identified as of special architectural or historic interest. Recognition and protection provide the platform for the development of management strategies that acknowledge that finding new uses for historic warehouses is the best means of securing their long-term future. The inevitable changes that come with adaptive reuse can be negotiated in the context of a shared appreciation of the special interest of warehouse buildings. This is what the planning system seeks to achieve through both planning and listed building control and the Government's best practice advice in relevant Planning Policy Guidance.

Although many of Liverpool's warehouses are individually distinctive, they have their greatest visual impact where they have survived in groups or among other related building types. In these instances, they help to create distinctive industrial or commercial landscapes, some of which have been recognised as having special character by the City Council, and designated as conservation areas. Such areas are legally protected, and change is managed by means of the Conservation Area Consent procedure. Hartley's warehouses around the Albert Dock represent this commercial landscape most powerfully, but there are other instances where significant groupings of historic buildings make a strong visual impact. The best concentrations of early survivals are to be found within central Liverpool, close to the site of Steers' Old Dock, the focal point for the development of the surrounding street pattern in the 18th century. Here, the Duke Street Conservation Area, embracing parts of Hanover Street, Henry Street, Seel Street and Bold Street, retains many early structures, which demonstrate the importance of the warehouse not only as a historic building type, but also as a signpost building. Steers' Dock has been lost (but survives at least in part below ground), but the warehouses and a small number of merchants' houses remain as proof of what formerly took place here. They are the physical evidence of the past without which we would have only maps and illustrations to aid our interpretation of this rapidly changing historic landscape.

The same holds true for other groups of warehouses in different parts of the city, representing later and different phases of development. Survivals in the Baltic Triangle, such as the warehouses that form part of Heap's Rice Mill, now stand in relative isolation, separated from both the waterfront and the city centre by new developments. Further to the south, however, around Bridgewater Street and Jamaica Street (Fig 47), and in some pockets to the north of the centre, to either side of Great

Howard Street, sufficient warehouses remain to reflect the formerly commercial character of these areas set just outside the barrier represented by Hartley's dock wall. In the city centre, particularly in the grid of streets linking the principal routes from Lime Street to the waterfront – Dale Street, Tithebarn Street and Victoria Street – warehouses are close neighbours of some of the city's most prestigious 19th-century public and commercial buildings. What might now appear as an incongruous presence is in fact powerful evidence of how integrated the warehouse had become in the warp and weft of the city, and of how widespread the warehousing business became.

The key to future success in the conservation of warehouses lies not solely in the tools to protect them. These will be effective only if they are used in the context of a shared appreciation of their historical and architectural qualities and of what these qualities contribute to the city's environment. If this can be allied to creative thinking to identify appropriate new uses, then there is every chance that these robust buildings will make an important contribution to the physical and economic rebirth of the city.

There are, of course, many models for emulation, not least in Liverpool itself. The repair and refurbishment of the Albert Dock provided a flagship example of how one of the world's greatest historic dock ensembles could be reused, and other dock warehouses – at Wapping and Waterloo Docks – have made very successful residential conversions, but continue nevertheless to give an important historic element to these revitalised waterfront areas. Inspiration can also be taken from abroad, where other great port cities – the 'villes portuaires' – are dealing with a similar legacy of historic warehouse buildings. In Marseille, for instance, the imaginative conversion of the enormous fireproof complex originally known as the 'Grand Entrepôt de la Compagnie des Docks' provides us with an outstanding French example of the potential of warehouse buildings for adaptive reuse. Built between 1859 and 1868 to the designs of the company's engineer, Desplaces, at La Joliette, 'Les Docks', as they are now known, comprise a seven-storey, 365-metre-long complex of four linked secure courtyards, converted to mixed commercial use between 1991 and 2001 (Fig 48). The architect

Fig 47 *Bridgewater Street: the upper part of the street still retains its canyon-like form. [AA045310]*

Fig 48 *An internal courtyard forming part of the 'Grand Entrepôt de la Compagnie des Docks' at la Joliette, Marseille, France, recently converted to new commercial uses by the architect Eric Castaldi.* [DP002422]

for this project, Eric Castaldi, visited the Albert Dock while preparing his designs, just as the creators of Marseille's mid-19th-century dock developments had come to Liverpool to see Hartley's works.

Most of Liverpool's warehouses are much less spectacular than these great dock buildings, but the city's smaller structures show equally successful examples of conversions to offices and housing (Fig 49a–c). A number of warehouses in the Duke Street Conservation Area have been converted, but they retain their distinctive architectural character externally and act as an inspiration for nearby new build. The result is the creation of an exciting urban landscape, part old and reflecting the city's history, part new and making a strong contribution of its own. The mix of old and new in such areas is of critical importance. Where new buildings are to be placed close to historic warehouses, care must be taken to ensure that the setting of the warehouse and its place in the local hierarchy of buildings have been respected: the height, massing and location on plot of the proposed new development are vital ingredients of successful schemes.

An understanding of the architectural character of warehouses is crucial to the success of schemes of conversion. Externally, most significant detail is confined to the street frontage of the building, and is represented by its gabled profile, the loading doorways, entrance doorways and hoist beams, and the window openings to the storage floors and the stairway (Fig 50a–e). The functional details of the elevations, such as fireproof doors, harness mountings and hoist canopies (sometimes showing the date of construction), are also significant. The brickwork and roofing materials also contribute a great deal to the special character of warehouses. Most buildings are of characteristic plain mud-brown brick, probably sourced locally, but many have some modest polychrome effect, with bands of white, yellow, blue (from Dudley) or hard red (probably Ruabon and Accrington) brick. Roof coverings, where original, are almost invariably of Welsh slate. Internally, the heavy floors, with beams, joists and timber or cast-iron supports, and the timber roof structures provide the main structural elements, with added interest given by the narrow stairway, the 'jigger loft', sometimes with its original hoist, and shutters to windows.

a

Fig 49 *Conversions from warehouse to dwelling:*

(a) 81 Henry Street [AA045311];

(b) 6 Fleet Street, where the new takes its form from the old [AA045312]; and

(c) 15 Argyle Street, in the restored Campbell Square area of town [AA041748].

b

c

a

b

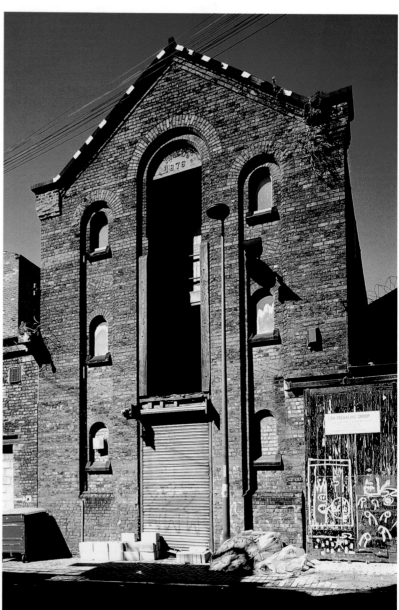

c

d

e

Fig 50 *The character of warehouses. External details:*

(a) *timber loading door and hoist beam at 22 College Lane [AA045314];*

(b) *iron loading door and hoist beam, Kitchen Street [AA045338];*

(c) *decorative brickwork at 45 Henry Street [AA045337];*

(d) *polychrome brickwork at 14–18 Henry Street [AA045336]; and*

(e) *polychrome brickwork and metal window frame at Phoenix Oil Mill, Jamaica Street [AA045340].*

Proposals for change of use can respect these elements of the building. The warehouse is not a complex building type, and its open-plan interior offers scope for reinterpretation that need not compromise its distinctive character and appearance. The parameters for change will vary from building to building, according to its individual identity and the kinds of new uses envisaged. There is no prescribed 'best practice' formula for change of use proposals, but guidance is appropriate in the interests of defining more clearly where change is likely to be acceptable in areas of greatest sensitivity. This guidance anticipates some of the requirements of the planning system, but also acknowledges issues of concern to those who wish to develop proposals for change.

New uses inevitably bring with them the need for alteration. The conservation challenge is to achieve a balanced outcome, on the one hand satisfying the needs of the user and the requirements of building regulations, and on the other respecting the integrity of the building. The first tier of design issues is likely to concern the treatment of external openings and the need for internal subdivision. Secondary issues involve consideration of the means of providing access between floors, security and safety, acoustics and insulation, and the routing of ducting, plumbing and electricity networks, together with matters associated with multiple occupancy. Alongside the proposals for change will be the issues related to the repair and conservation of the historic fabric of the building – the repair and repointing of brickwork, repairs to slate roof coverings, external doors and shutters, hoist beams, existing stairways, and original floor and roof systems. Done well, this work enhances the building; done poorly, character is lost, perhaps forever.

The reinterpretation of exterior elevations so as to maximise the benefit of existing openings will provide the most acceptable means of access and of lighting the interior of the building. The glazing of the former loading door openings can provide large windows or glazed door openings, which can be set at, or recessed behind, the former door position. The retention of the loading doors as external shutters will both reduce the impact of the alterations to the openings and retain original building components. Most warehouse frontages are free of projections, apart from the hoist beams. In some buildings, the tiered loading doorways and hoist beam are set within a full-height recess. Proposals for new openings, for the infilling of recessed doorways, and for additions that project beyond the building frontage are unlikely to be supported.

Some warehouses have exposed side and rear walls, often with original windows. These secondary elevations may offer scope for carefully proportioned additional openings. Where this is not possible, rooms that do not require natural light may be placed in the darker spaces. The creation of light wells and the use of windows in the plane of the roof may be supportable in particularly restricted circumstances, provided that such alterations are appropriately detailed, and their design respects the character of the building.

Internal planning raises further design issues. The most easily accepted adaptations will be those that retain the warehouse's open-plan interiors (Fig 51), but many proposals will include the insertion of internal divisions into these large spaces. Careful design can reduce the need for subdivision, and non-structural, reversible alterations and the use of glazed or semi-glazed partitions can lessen the impact of such changes. Similarly sensitive treatment of floor, hoist loft and roof structures can ensure the continued visibility of those features that are most indicative of the building's former use. In some instances the original stair is unlikely to be adequate for the new uses envisaged, but can be retained in a secondary role alongside an appropriately designed new stairway.

The responsibility for guiding the future of Liverpool's historic warehouses is shared among a number of agencies. Presiding over the system of planning consent, listed building consent and conservation area consent applications is Liverpool City Council, which shares with English Heritage a commitment to seeing warehouses play a dynamic role in the city's rebirth through regeneration. Of greatest importance, however, are those owners, architects, surveyors and developers who take the risks, provide the funding and prepare the schemes for conversion. It is their vision, combining hard-headed business sense with a care for the historic environment, that, ultimately, will determine what part the city's

Fig 51 *Loft living in a converted warehouse in Argyle Street: here the space remains undivided; natural light streams in from the loading door and windows in the front wall; and the hoist has been retained as a feature, linking the space with its original use. [© Beetham Organization]*

warehouses will play in the future. The key, beyond doubt, is partnership. Informed by good understanding, motivated by a desire to give new life to this diagnostic building type, convinced that warehouses should continue to give special character to one of England's great cities, English Heritage, the City Council and the private sector can work together to hand on a precious resource to future generations.

References and further reading

Aikin, J 1795 *A Description of the Country from Thirty to Forty Miles round Manchester*. London

Anon 1820 *The Stranger in Liverpool*, 6 edn. Liverpool: T Kaye

Boult, J 1869 'The structural requirements of the Fire Prevention Acts'. *Proceedings of the Liverpool Architectural and Archaeological Society* (16 Dec 1868), 73–90

Gaskell, E 1848 *Mary Barton: A Tale of Manchester Life* (edited by Angus Easson, 1993). Halifax: Ryburn

Gawthrop, H 1861 *Fraser's Guide to Liverpool and Birkenhead*. London and Liverpool

Hughes, Q 1999 *Liverpool: City of Architecture*, 2 edn. Liverpool: Bluecoat Press

Jarvis, A and Smith, K (eds) 1999 *Albert Dock: Trade and Technology*. Liverpool: National Museums and Galleries on Merseyside

Liverpool City Council 2003 *Liverpool Maritime Mercantile City* (Nomination of Liverpool – Maritime Mercantile City for inscription on the World Heritage List)

Moorman, M 1969 *The Letters of William and Dorothy Wordsworth, vol 2: The Middle Years, part 1: 1806–1811*. Oxford: Clarendon Press

Picton, J A 1875 *Memorials of Liverpool: Historical and Topographical*, 2 edn, 2 vols. London: Longmans, Green

Ritchie-Noakes, N 1984 *Liverpool's Historic Waterfront: The World's First Mercantile Dock System* (RCHME, Merseyside County Museums). London: HMSO

Troughton, T 1810 *The History of Liverpool*. London and Liverpool

Front cover *Rum storage in Clarence Warehouses. The modern use of this building illustrates how many warehouses were used in the 19th century. [AA045330]*

Inside front cover *Button Street, now a fashionable shopping street in the centre of the city, is lined on one side with substantial warehouses. Built in the 1860s, they were occupied principally by provision merchants and wholesale grocers. [AA045282]*

Inside back cover *Map of Liverpool, showing the main warehouse locations.*

Back cover flap *Poster from Clarence Warehouses. [AA045329]*

Back cover *Jamaica Street sign. [AA045341]*